Stripes and Spots

Written by Jo Windsor

Stripes

3

The tiger has stripes.

The zebra has stripes.

The snail has stripes.

The bee has stripes.

Spots

9

The leopard has spots.

The giraffe has spots.

The beetle has spots.

The dog has spots.

14

Index

Guide Notes

Title: **Stripes and Spots**

Stage: Emergent – Magenta

Genre: Nonfiction (Expository)

Approach: Guided Reading

Processes: Thinking Critically, Exploring Language, Processing Information

Written and Visual Focus: Photographs (static images), Illustrations, Index

READING THE TEXT

Tell the children that this book is about some animals that have stripes or spots.

Talk to them about what is on the front cover. Read the title and the author.

Focus the children's attention on the index and talk about the animals that are in this book.

"Walk" through the book, focusing on the photographs and talk about the different animals and whether they have stripes or spots.

Read the text together.

THINKING CRITICALLY
(sample questions)
- What other animals have stripes or spots?
- How do stripes or spots help animals?

EXPLORING LANGUAGE
(ideas for selection)

Terminology
Title, cover, author, photographs, illustrations

Vocabulary
Interest words: stripes, spots, tiger, zebra, snail, bee, leopard, giraffe, beetle, dog
High-frequency words: the, has